Caring for New Christians

A training course for nurture group leaders

GW00633324

About this book

What is *Caring for New Christians*?

Caring for New Christians is a training programme to help churches
establish new Christians in their faith and in their local Christian
community. It provides material for a **five-session training event**
which will equip existing church members to lead or be core
members of small groups engaged in a **six-week nurture course**,
Living as a Christian. So this book has two quite distinct parts: the
training programme; and leaders' notes for the nurture course.

The programme was first put together for "Mission England" from
material by John Mallison and Eddie Gibbs. The publishers are
grateful to the original authors for their continued willingness to
have the material used in this way. The resulting *Caring for New
Christians* programme proved to meet a real need in churches of
differing theological persuasion and practice, even among those who
had been church-goers for many years. Such was the enthusiasm
that the material has been further revised to produce a manual
which can be used by local churches independently of any larger
event.

What will I need?

To run the training programme and the nurture course you will need
certain basics— **people** and **materials**.

People

> At least one person (maybe yourself) who can run the training
> sessions
>
> At least two or three others who can attend the training and be
> leaders or core members of nurture groups (see **page 10**)
>
> At least two or three who have expressed a desire to learn
> about the Christian faith or who have recently decided to
> follow Christ

Materials

> *Caring for New Christians* for everyone who will attend the
> training sessions—leaders and core members
>
> *Living as a Christian* for everyone (including leaders) who will
> be in the nurture groups
>
> Luke's Gospel, in a modern translation such as the *Good News
> Bible*, for everyone in the nurture groups. These can be

obtained from your local Christian bookshop or direct from
Bible Society

How does it work?

No programme can work without people—in this case those willing
to be leaders and working (core) members, and those wanting to
begin living as Christians. If you don't have those basic ingredients,
you have more work (and praying) to do before beginning the
programme.

The scheme will work best in a church or a group (youth, young
mums, *etc*.) where several people are committed to seeing
individuals come to believe in Jesus Christ and to follow him, and to
bringing those individuals into the local believing community. You
may be planning some special or regular events to talk about the
person of Christ, or perhaps people have naturally been drawn to
the group because they are wanting to follow Christ. A group of
Christians trained to share their faith and encourage others, and a
short course covering basics of Christian belief and living can help
bring a work of God to fruition in a way that is exhilarating for all
concerned. You will need to talk to other Christians, share your
enthusiasm and enlist their support; under normal circumstances,
this isn't something to be tackled on your own. Ideally it should be
under the direction of the local church leadership.

You can run groups for young Christians whenever you need them
in your church life, but if you are undertaking any special
evangelistic activity, do include planning and training for the groups
as part of your preparation for evangelism. You need to have them
"ready to run" when they are needed.

When you have a group keen to care for new Christians, you will
need to organize the training programme. There are five sessions,
each designed to last about 75 minutes, which can be run on one
night a week for five weeks, or at a weekend (*e.g.* on Friday night
and on Saturday morning and afternoon). Choose whichever
pattern suits you best. It is worth training as many people as are
willing to come; it will be a stimulus to their faith and will mean
you have a pool of trained people to draw from in the future.

There may be occasions, however, when you need to "go it alone"
and, having read the training material, start a small nurture group
with two or three new Christians and you as leader. This won't be
as satisfactory because new Christians will miss being introduced to
the Christian community, and you will miss the support of others.
But it may sometimes be necessary.

At other times it may be difficult to get established Christians together for the training sessions. It is possible to run the nurture groups without the training programme, simply giving training materials to leaders and core members, but again you will all miss the important elements of experience and relationships. For leaders too, the Christian faith is more than "head knowledge"!

What exactly is a nurture group?

In recent years small groups have begun to play a significant role in bringing new life to the Christian community.

For many in the church this has come as a completely new idea. But small groups are not new at all. Our Lord built his ministry around two dynamic small groups. He equipped the twelve disciples, with the inner core of three (Peter, James, and John), to become the foundation of his church. The early church followed this plan, as have some of the most important movements in the history of the church. And today many Christians are realizing again that all ministry in the church is an extension of Christ's ministry: we should take seriously not only the message our Lord proclaimed but also the strategy he used.

There are now many types of small groups being used effectively in the church for outreach, nurture, growth, fellowship, service, planning, and many other purposes.

Nurture groups are short-term groups, usually lasting six to eight weeks, which provide support to help new disciples of Christ begin their life together in a caring fellowship of Christian love.

Training course objectives

1   To learn the basic skills for leading small groups.
2   To be alert to the felt needs of enquirers and new Christians.
3   To be able to lead a six-session nurture course.
4   To be effective in incorporating new Christians into the local church.

The need for nurture

The Bible uses many different word-pictures when it speaks of beginning to live as a Christian. Christians have become "a new being" (2 Corinthians 5.17), "God's children" (Romans 8.15); they are those who have turned to God (Acts 3.19) and been "born again" (1 Peter 1.23).

Jesus uses the image of being born again in his conversation with Nicodemus (John 3.1-21). Like new-born human babies, those who are born again spiritually need special care to help them become established. Small nurture groups can provide a warm, personal atmosphere in which they can feel accepted as persons and make a good start in their new-found faith.

Some new Christians are very unsure of themselves and if they have recently made a public commitment to Christ in a church or meeting, they may be feeling a little embarrassed about it. They may already have been mocked by their friends and workmates. For others, making a commitment may have been the conscious culmination of a long journey towards faith in Jesus Christ.

How do new Christians feel?

Within a few days of having made a conscious decision to follow Christ, new Christians are likely to enter a period of **uncertainty**.

- They will begin to see some of the **implications** of their decision in terms of changed attitudes and relationships
- They may have to **explain** their new outlook and commitment to other people
- They may look with high expectations at other Christians or churches . . . and sometimes they will be **disappointed**
- They may be baffled by the differences and controversies within the Christian church and be unable to decide which voice to listen to

This may not be so traumatic for those with a church background, or those who already have Christian friends. If they made a commitment at an evangelistic event, it was probably an occasion when they declared publicly an intention to follow Christ, which had been slowly growing. They will have made their decision with a clearer idea that they are committing themselves to

- live in obedience to the commands of Christ
- becoming a functioning part of the local church with which they are already in contact

For those with little or no church background, however, first impressions can be confusing. If they made their response to Christ at a public meeting

- they were part of a crowd, which provided a sense of security
- they were listening to a gifted speaker, possibly with a great reputation
- they may have been in familiar surroundings—"on their own pitch"
- they may have been involved in an impressive programme with a variety of activities and powerful personalities

After that, the local church may come as something of an anticlimax.

How do local churches respond to new Christians?

Some churches just don't know what to do with new Christians, who are full of questions and their new experience of Christ.

There are several possibilities. They might

Ignore them

Some churches can appear to be completely uninterested.

Interrogate them

Some are suspicious and defensive and will want newcomers to pass a doctrinal test before being accepted. The result is that new Christians feel threatened rather than welcomed and accepted by the local church.

Deflate them

The new Christian's decision and experience may be belittled or explained away by those who are uncomfortable with radical changes or sudden "conversion" experiences in people's lives.

Isolate them

New Christians may be welcomed but are then left to fend for themselves. This is like expecting a new-born baby to make its own way in the world.

Incorporate them

This will happen when the church
understands how new Christians feel
and how to provide what they need.
The leaders will realize that new
Christians need

- to be helped through their traumas
- to relate to other Christians
- to be provided with basic lessons for
  spiritual survival and growth
- to learn alongside other new Christians

From "day one" new Christians must

- feel wanted
- be personally introduced to people who share their
  exhilaration and recognize the significance of their decision to
  follow Christ
- have a good experience of the local church

Quality does not depend on quantity. Even a small church can be
attractive to the newcomer if it is really welcoming.

How does the nurture group course fit in?

The six sessions of the nurture group course, *Living as a Christian*
(pages 29–45), have been specially designed to enable new
Christians to start building relationships with one another, learn
together, and worship and pray together. These are the elements
they need in order to become established. The course is intentionally
as much to do with relationships as study.

You should be able to identify the following objectives in the
nurture course, some of them in each session:

1 **TO PROVIDE OPPORTUNITIES FOR GROUP MEMBERS
   TO GET TO KNOW ONE ANOTHER**

   The aim is to establish deepening relationships without forcing
   the pace. Sometimes the sessions include talking in pairs and
   sometimes there is opportunity to talk with the whole group.

2 **TO ENSURE THAT SPIRITUAL FOUNDATIONS HAVE
   BEEN PROPERLY LAID**

   Those still troubled by failure and sin need to accept Christ's
   forgiveness; those still unsure need to be assured of the
   presence of the Holy Spirit; all need to know new life and
   strength and learn to maintain a relationship with Jesus Christ.

3   TO ENCOURAGE REGULAR BIBLE READING

Luke's Gospel will be used in the groups and it will be good for individuals to read through the Gospel on their own between sessions. A plan is provided in the back of this book and some editions of Luke's Gospel also contain a reading guide.

Personal Bible reading is linked with group sharing to reinforce and help apply the lessons being learnt. By the time the group finishes, new disciples will know how to look things up in the Bible and will have studied a few significant passages for beginners in the faith. Learning to pick out the main points in Bible passages and to see how the Bible applies to daily living will be key experiences for new Christians.

4   TO DEVELOP CONFIDENCE IN BEGINNING TO PRAY ALOUD

The new Christians should hear others pray and, starting with silent prayer and simple word and sentence prayers, build up enough confidence to begin to pray aloud themselves.

5   TO ENABLE GROUP MEMBERS TO BEGIN TO SHARE THEIR FAITH

New Christians are often the most effective witnesses—both to non-Christians and older Christians. The course will encourage everyone to begin to talk to others about Christ and to share with the group any difficulties they have had.

Group work

We all need plenty of practice in getting to know new people and remembering what it feels like to come in "from the outside". So the training course includes some of the exercises from the nurture group course.

There is sometimes a tendency for mature and well taught Christians to underestimate the importance of the "Getting acquainted" parts of the course. But these are especially important for those with little or no church background.

Leaders will also need to be very familiar with the nurture group material. So the training course includes group participation in the Bible studies to be used in your nurture groups.

- Divide into groups of 6
- See "Getting acquainted" (page 31)
- As these same groups will be used throughout the training course **decide on a leader** for your group

Nurturing new disciples

New Christians should be invited to join a nurture group as soon as possible after they have decided to follow Christ. It usually causes less confusion if the group can be held in the same place throughout the nurture course.

What is a nurture group?

We have seen that new Christians have special needs. The nurture group is a gathering of people, some experienced Christians, some new Christians, where those needs can be met in a caring, supportive environment.

- New Christians are helped to take some first steps and are given some very basic "food" and support. Relationships with their new-found Lord and other members of their new "family" are carefully developed in an atmosphere of care and concern. (See "How does the nurture group course fit in?", pages 7–8.)

- Although the Bible will play a very important part in the group, the aim is not simply to do Bible study. The group will also try to care for and encourage new Christians, making them feel wanted and accepted. It will be a place for new Christians to get to know others, share experiences, and ask questions.

- A nurture group is also like a **bridge** helping new Christians into the wider fellowship of a local church. The group is a smaller version of the larger church. It is important that new disciples are not pressured to join other groups or organizations within the church at this stage; they need to become established first.

What a nurture group is not

1   IT IS NOT A LECTURE
where one person talks and
the rest listen

2   IT IS NOT A PANEL OF EXPERTS
where those who know are probed by the beginners to get "the answers"

3   IT IS NOT A DEBATE

with several people talking at
one another from different viewpoints
to see who can win
Instead
- the Bible is the authority
- the Holy Spirit is the teacher
- the leader simply helps the group
  to define and achieve its goals
- it is up to **each** member to develop and apply Bible truths to meet the needs of the group members

Who should go to the nurture group?

Personal, individual help is important. If possible, every new Christian should be linked with a "helper" who will be responsible for encouraging and supporting them (and maybe several others) in Christian living.

The "helpers" are also the **core members** responsible for inviting the new Christians to the nurture group and going with them to the meetings. A mixed group like this can stimulate both new and older disciples.

Stimulus and encouragement among the leaders and core members can be promoted by making it a priority to meet together for mutual support and prayer before and during the period of the groups.

Ideally the group should contain between **7 and 12** and the newcomers should outnumber the core members. Don't overload the group with mature Christians as the new disciples may not participate freely.

Who can be a core member?

"Helpers" who are assigned to new Christians must
- have a living, growing relationship with Jesus Christ
- be honest, sensitive, and able to listen, with a genuine concern for people
- have a reasonable working knowledge of the Bible
- be committed to one another and loyal to the local church

- feel called by God and be appointed by the church to the task of nurturing new Christians
- be able to relate to the problems of those completely new to Christianity (this may be hard for some who have been in a Christian environment for years)
- be able to keep confidences (the personalities, backgrounds, and needs of group members should not be discussed in the wider church)
- see themselves as learning alongside the new Christian— humble, open, and aware of their own need for continual growth

In short, they are people on the way to becoming like their Lord— but who know they have not yet arrived!

Getting together

1   WORKING WITH CLUSTERS OF GROUPS TOGETHER

There may be occasions when those who have completed the training programme do not feel confident to lead the whole nurture course. In this case, the groups could meet together on church premises. The minister and/or some experienced lay people could lead the meetings, with most work and sharing being done in small groups, led by the trained leaders. If you do this, be sure you have individual seating so that you can split up easily into groups.

2   COMBINED GET-TOGETHERS

There is often value in holding a combined meeting of all those who have become Christians or are wanting to find out more about being Christian along with the "helpers". An informal evening is best, with time to get to know one another and for sharing and worship. Do not make an initial meeting like this too long. Refreshments or a light supper would make a good ending to the occasion.

This combined meeting may be used to launch the home-based nurture groups or to conclude them, or both.

3   ALL-AGE OR PEER GROUPS?

There is an increasing emphasis in Christian education upon intergenerational work—a mixed age group with all working together. This is a healthy trend away from the division into youth and adults, and the splitting up of the family which has happened in most church programmes. Some churches may therefore choose to run their nurture groups on an all-age basis.

However, for the small and more intimate group such as a nurture group there can be value in dividing people into peer groups, particularly where there are extremes of culture and background amongst the members. For example, some older folk may feel very threatened if put in a group of noisy, boisterous youth or punk rockers! It would be best for people with a similar background to struggle together with the problems of witness and lifestyle. For example, secondary school young people can discuss the particular situations they face at school (though one or two mature Christians amongst the core members would help).

One age group that needs special thought is that of children (*i.e.* up to 11 years old). Small groups are of great benefit for this age group but they need to be of a different style. It is important that children have some of the most experienced and capable leaders in their group and not just one or two keen young people who will be able to look after them.

Planning of the programme for a children's group must be undertaken carefully, particularly bearing in mind that children need variety to cater for their inability to concentrate for long on one point.

In organizing this group

- keep the parents fully informed (perhaps invite them to an adult group)
- arrange a time that is convenient for children
- include some activity in the programme
- include memory verses, quizzes, and songs in the programme
- use visual aids whenever possible
- incorporate them in the life of the church, including existing groups for their age

Group work

- Sharing—talk about commitment (page 30)
- Group Bible study: Luke 23.39-49 (page 37)

(Note: In each of the group studies during the training course try to see the passage through the eyes of a new Christian.)

- Prayer—pray now for the new Christians you will nurture, whether you know them or not, and for sensitivity and awareness of their needs.

What new Christians need to know

Our emphasis in this book is on building relationships and sharing new experiences and insights amongst those who have recently begun to follow Christ.

But new Christians also need to grasp more firmly what it is that God has done for them through Christ and what he asks in response from them. The *Living as a Christian* nurture course takes up the themes of

- Beginning
- Being sure
- Growing
- Being obedient
- Being established
- Continuing

and deals with them in a very practical and personal way from the point of view of the new Christian.

A basic outline of the Christian gospel, with illustrations, is on pages 33—35. It is designed to be used in the first nurture group session, to reinforce the essentials for new Christians. Core members should all be familiar with the material and leaders need to be able to present it to the group, taking no more than 15 minutes.

Dealing with questions

Just as young children are full of questions, so are young Christians. It will be most helpful if core members of nurture groups have already made themselves familiar with short, basic introductions to the Christian faith and life, so that they can give appropriate help to the new Christians in their group.

There are many such books available cheaply and representing different church traditions. A selection is given in the Resources list (page 47) but you may know of another more appropriate to your church.

In addition, because new Christians are often enthusiastic but untaught, they may share their new-found faith with friends but then be unable to answer the questions they ask. The group can help provide direction to new Christians in answering these questions. Paul Little's *How To Give Away Your Faith* (IVP) suggests some of the key questions asked by non-Christians.

Here we shall restrict ourselves to setting out some of the most important points that new Christians need to know. Core members need to be familiar with them and watch out for them as they arise in the course of conversation. If any of them fail to emerge and you think that they are particularly important for some individuals to grasp, look for an opportunity to raise the questions yourself.

1   HOW CHRIST HAS SECURED MY FORGIVENESS

- I am accepted by God not because he has considered me good enough but because Christ died to be my Saviour. God has pronounced me forgiven because Christ paid the debt I owe to God for having lived my life in selfish rebellion against him. I could never have paid the debt on my own.

- Because of what Christ has done and because I believe in him, God has adopted me as his child and I will not be rejected even though I do wrong in the future.

- The way I live does matter, however. If I knowingly disobey God I am creating a barrier in our relationship. I must learn to ask him to forgive me as soon as I am aware of having done anything to displease him. I need to learn, too, to ask his Holy Spirit to help me resist temptations and be obedient to God.
  Useful Bible verses: John 3.16; Philippians 1.6; 1 John 1.9

2   HOW CHRIST LIVES IN ME BY HIS SPIRIT

- I can know the presence of Christ because the Holy Spirit makes me aware of Jesus in my life.

- He works in my life to make my character more like Christ's.

- He helps and strengthens me to serve Jesus in the world.
  John 14.15-31; 16.5-15; Galatians 5.22-23; Acts 1.8

3   HOW GOD SPEAKS TO ME THROUGH THE BIBLE

- By reading the Bible I can learn more about what God is like and how he deals with people.

- The Bible contains many different parts, written over many years to different kinds of people facing a whole range of "real life" situations.

- It is a practical book which can help me in my own life to set right priorities and make the right decisions in following Christ.

- Because the Bible is God's Word I can trust it and base my actions upon it. God's promises can give me great strength and confidence as a Christian.
  Psalm 119.9-16; Matthew 4.4; 2 Timothy 3.14-17

4 HOW GOD INVITES ME TO SPEAK TO HIM

- For two people to establish a relationship they need to spend time together and to talk with one another. This applies to my relationship with God, too.

- Just as a caring and responsible human parent would, God wants me as his child to be honest and open and to tell him everything that is on my mind. With God, nothing is too trivial to mention; nothing is so awful that I need to hide it.

- He likes me to be quiet sometimes, too: to think about what he has said to me in the Bible, and to see if he wants to say anything directly to me. I need to listen as well as to talk.
  Luke 5.15-16; Matthew 6.5-15; Philippians 4.6-7; 1 John 5.14-15

5 HOW CHRIST WANTS TO HAVE THE CENTRAL PLACE IN MY LIFE

- Being a Christian means giving Christ control of my life. There may be a lot for him to clear up and sort out. He is concerned about every part: my home life, where I work, my friendships and leisure interests.

- He died so that I could live a fuller and richer life, as God intended me to.

- He has a plan for my life and I must maintain a close relationship with him in order to follow the right path. He will guide me if I ask him.
  Galatians 2.20; John 10.10b; Colossians 2.6-7; 3.1-4

6 HOW CHRIST WANTS ME TO SHARE HIS LOVE AND THE GOOD NEWS ABOUT HIM

- His love is for everyone. He wants me to share the Good News with others.

- But I must be careful not to "ram it down people's throats" because that will only make them "switch off". God's Holy Spirit is the only one who can convince people; it isn't my job to try to do it for him!

- Wherever I go Jesus is with me. So I am always a witness to him by the kind of person I am, the attitudes I show, the things I do and what I say.
  Acts 1.8; 2 Corinthians 6.6-7; 1 Peter 3.15

7 HOW THE CHURCH WILL HELP ME TO GROW IN MY CHRISTIAN LIFE

- Christ has not saved me in isolation—I am now part of his

church. He wants me to demonstrate that by becoming a
functioning part of a local church.

● In fellowship with other Christians I can be supported,
encouraged, and my personal needs and those of my family
can be met. The church provides the context in which I live the
whole of my life.

● Each person in the church is an important and valued member
with a role to play. Through his Holy Spirit, God gives us the
gifts and abilities we need to serve him in the church and in the
local community.

Ephesians 4.1-16; Romans 12.1-8; 1 Peter 2.9-10

Group work

● "Getting to know each other" (page 38)
● Sharing—"What has God been doing in your life?"
(page 38)
● Group Bible study: Luke 8.4-15 (page 39)

Leading a nurture group

Responsibilities of a leader

1   ESTABLISH THE CORE GROUP

Arrange a meeting of your core members to discuss and pray together about your nurturing responsibilities. Find out about individual backgrounds and try to identify gifts. (If this is a new idea to you, books in the Resources list on page 47 will help.)

2   ENSURE THAT THE "HELPER" SCHEME IS WORKING

Make sure that core members make their links with new Christians and that personal invitations are given and arrangements made to meet newcomers.

3   LIAISE WITH THE MINISTER

Make sure you have adequate information about the new Christians in your group and report back on the progress of the group and any particular problems.

4   SUPERVISE THE PRACTICAL ARRANGEMENTS

A home is often the best venue because of the intimacy and warmth which it provides. Decide in advance who will answer doorbells, telephones, and children. You should avoid venues which will make people feel uncomfortable or where the group will be unduly disturbed by other family members. In some situations a comfortable room on church premises may be best. Make someone responsible for refreshments and for getting the room ready. Don't forget important details like lighting and ventilation. If people are too hot or too cold, left without fresh air, unable to see books (or each other!) clearly, or feel that they are "in the spotlight", they will not be able to relax and concentrate on the session.

5   MONITOR THE EFFECTIVENESS OF THE GROUP

Keep your goals and expectations (see page 7) firmly in mind, both for the new Christians and the functioning of the group as a whole. (It is often good to write out the aims of each section you prepare.) Make sure the group remains outward-looking and does not become a private clique. Take remedial action and, if necessary, get help in any problem areas.

**6   ENSURE THAT MEMBERS HAVE THE HELP AND ADVICE
THEY NEED**

Keep the personal needs of group members uppermost in your
mind. Be ready to help core members individually outside
group meetings so that they can play their part effectively.
You may sometimes want to direct them to someone with
more experience. They in turn should be giving individual help
to the new Christians, but there may be times when you need
to be involved here also.

7   KEEP A RECORD OF ATTENDANCE

This needs to be done discreetly, of course, but it will help
ensure that absentees are not overlooked. Encourage core
members to follow up any absent person before the next
session.

8   PRAY

Pray regularly and specifically for each member of the group.

Leaders' preparation before group sessions

1   It is important to be clear in your own mind what you want to
achieve in each group meeting, and for your expectations to
relate to the needs of the members. The objective is to achieve
these goals, not to follow the session outline to the last letter.
And don't forget to assess afterwards whether you achieved
your goals!

2   Read through the leader's guide for each session (pages 29—45
in this book) to be sure you understand exactly what to do.

3   The suggested activities for each of the six sessions are meant
to be a guide; feel free to use alternative activities if they
would suit the group better. Where there are optional
activities, decide which you will use and consider if you will
have to adapt them in any way.

4   Study the Bible passage thoroughly. You will find it helpful to
have access to a short commentary on Luke's Gospel so that
you can consult it in your preparation. You might like to have
one handy for the group to use too.

5   Try to absorb all this information yourself but don't expect to
use it all as you lead the group session. The watchword here is
"keep it simple".

6   Prepare some questions or activities to keep as a stand-by if
the discussion begins to flag at any stage.

7 You might want to write on a large sheet of paper (or on an acetate if an overhead projector will be available), or to duplicate any illustrations, questions, or Bible study instructions which group members will need and which are not in *Living as a Christian*.

8 Write a summary of the session to ensure that you are clear in your own mind what you want the session to achieve.

9 Have a timetable for the session which gives a balanced time allocation. A rough guide would be:

Group sharing   15—20 minutes
Bible study   45 minutes
Prayer   10 minutes

In addition:

● Some of the material in this guide has been taken from *Building Small Groups* and *Creative Ideas for Small Groups* by John Mallison (SU, 1981), which give guidelines and helps for small-group leaders. You will be better equipped for your leadership role if you are aware of some of the practical insights in these books. Others are in the Resources list on page 47.

● When group members are getting to the end of their individual reading of Luke's Gospel it will be helpful to have available copies of Bible reading programmes. Different schemes are published by Bible Reading Fellowship, Bible Society, Crusade for World Revival, International Bible Reading Association, Scripture Union, and others, and some churches have their own lectionaries covering the whole year.

At the meeting

Remember how important it is that new disciples have a good experience of a real, caring, concerned Christian community, where they will feel accepted and significant. Do everything you can to make the group meetings times for experiencing true Christian love. Use this as a checklist:

1 BE READY

● If possible, have some spare copies of the Bible in an easy-to-read, modern translation (preferably the *Good News Bible* or the *New International Version*). It will help if everyone has the same translation.

● If you are going to ask people to write things down, have a supply of paper and pencils.

- If your group is quite large, you could use name tags for the first two or three weeks to help everyone remember names. Use them if a new member joins the group part of the way through the course, too. Collect them in at the end of the session for use next time.
- Make sure everyone is welcomed and try to help individuals get to know the other members.
- It is good to serve a drink and maybe some light refreshments at the end of each session. This gives a relaxed atmosphere for further informal fellowship and you may find that the most open conversations happen at this stage of the proceedings. Ask your hosts to be responsible for this.

2   BE ORDERLY

- Begin and end on time. Don't let the session drag on.
- Involve others in leadership. Give appropriate leadership roles to core members in each session.
- Make the meeting interesting and lively. Keep the pace going and avoid long talks.

3   BE CLEAR

- Use visual aids whenever possible; they are a tremendous help in understanding and retaining the message. Simple sketches, phrases, and words are all that are needed. You could use
  —felt pens with sheets of newsprint, chart paper or wallpaper attached to a piece of hardboard with snap clips
  —chalk and a chalkboard
  —an overhead projector if one is available
- Keep things simple. Avoid using clichés or technical Christian words which may mean little or nothing to a newcomer to the faith. A useful exercise is to write down short and simply-worded definitions of words and phrases such as "conversion", "grace", "commitment", "discipleship", "Christian experience" and "Christian lifestyle".
- Don't swamp people with too much information; it will only confuse or discourage them and they won't retain it.

4   BE SENSITIVE

- Be sensitive to the needs of individuals—that means being ready to listen!
- Deal gently but firmly with dominant members. Help the group to resolve conflict by trying to identify the cause of the frustration and suggesting ways of meeting it.

- Maintain eye contact with individuals in the group as much as possible. Keep looking around but be careful not to appear to be focusing on one person for a response to a question.

- Sometimes problems will be raised in the group which can't be handled satisfactorily during the meeting. In that case the leader or core member should aim to help the individual concerned some time after the meeting.

- Think carefully before using hymns or choruses in the meetings. Singing can be especially embarrassing if your group is small. Most non-churchgoers will find the practice a little strange to begin with. If you do sing, choose your songs carefully and try to include some well-known, traditional ones, or those with familiar tunes, as well as modern, informal choruses. You may find that some members do not know any.

- Be aware that many newcomers will know little about the Christian faith and how to live with it. Most will not know how to read the Bible or how to pray. Concentrate on telling them **how**, not stressing that they **ought**. Many will have difficulty finding passages in the Bible. This is where it will be helpful if everyone is using the same version and preferably the same edition. You can then give the page number with the passage. Do everything possible to avoid embarrassment, and give people plenty of time.

5 BE ADAPTABLE

- Do not be anxious if you do not get through all the activities each week; you need not do *everything*. Vary your plan for the session if a special need emerges. If you omit a point which you think is important for the group, you can always fit it in the following week. You could even spend two sessions on one study.

- Be unshockable! Those with no church background may have no idea what is and isn't "acceptable" in Christian circles. Be ready to step into awkward situations.

- Do not allow differences in temperament to develop into personality conflicts.

6 BE STIMULATING

- Encourage questions. The new Christians will be trying to understand and absorb many new ideas. They will need opportunity and time to sort out these new thoughts. Asking questions and talking about how their faith affects their life will be invaluable, so be patient with them.

- Emphasize that the Christian life is a growing experience. Remember that understanding and commitment are both things that grow. Don't expect them to be completely developed at the beginning.
- Demonstrate by personal example how to share experiences with others in the group. Allow plenty of time for members to share their own new experiences—don't fill every silence with your own words! This will help new Christians gain confidence in expressing their faith.

7 BE ENCOURAGING
- Encourage shy members to participate, but don't force them. Help them to know that it is all right to have a problem and to talk about it.
- Be careful not to put pressure on people to conform to *your* ideas of Christian lifestyle. This could inhibit openness and sharing, or even stop people coming. Give new Christians time to grow as the Word of God speaks to them.
- Aim to develop the corporate prayer life of the group but keep your praying simple—remember how you felt the first time you prayed with others.
- Help the group to appreciate silence, too—particularly being silent in God's presence.

Leading the discussion

A leader can help to create a good discussion.

- **ASK GUIDING QUESTIONS**

  A good question
  —requires more than a "yes" or "no" answer
  —is clearly stated
  —is short and to the point
  —is put in a non-threatening manner

  Guiding questions can
  —**define:** "What do we mean by . . .?"
  —**illustrate:** "How does this relate to our lives today?"
  —**personalize and apply:** "Has anyone experienced this?"
  —**relate back to Scripture:** "Is there anything in the Bible that supports this idea?" "If we turn to _____ (give page number if possible) what does the Bible say about this?"

- **CLARIFY**
  —when the discussion is in danger of becoming too involved,

or bogged down, or you are beginning to chase "red herrings"

—when someone uses difficult concepts or theological jargon. Ask the group "What do we mean by . . .?"

- **SUMMARIZE**

  At the end of a discussion which has taken in several comments from members, try to list the main ideas for the group to remember. You could invite someone else to do it of course, by saying, "How would you summarize what we have learnt about . . ."

Problem people and what to do about them

1 THE TALKATIVE

always speaking, never allowing space for others to speak

- Ask, "What does someone else think?"
- Give them the job of summarizing particular discussions so that they **have** to listen to others
- Talk to them privately about the problem

2 THE DOMINEERING

whose voice tends to "win" over all others, appearing to brush other people aside

- Challenge them by putting an alternative viewpoint
- Ask for other suggestions
- Break into pairs or "buzz groups" of three so that everyone has the opportunity to express a viewpoint

3 THE SILENT

who never contribute anything to the group discussion

- Try to find out the reason for the silence. Is it shyness? Reflection? Sullenness? Do they not understand?
- Give them opportunities by asking, "Does anyone want to add anything here?" or "How about those who haven't said anything so far?"
- Take time to "bring them out" privately, outside the meeting. Personal interest and encouragement can make all the difference

4 THE INSECURE

so unsure of themselves they would tend to say, "I don't know" to every question, just so they didn't give the "wrong" answer

- Choose an area where you know they have a contribution to make and invite them to speak
- When they do volunteer a response express appreciation on behalf of the group

5 THE NEGATIVE

who get attention by deliberately standing out against others

- They may secretly be very unsure of themselves and be testing whether the group really accepts them
- Try allowing them to express their negative feelings and responding warmly and positively to them as people
- Make a point, sometimes, of asking for *positive* contributions
- If the situation does not improve, and particularly if they have hurt others in the group, confront them with the problem— out of the meeting if at all possible.

6 THE "PRICKLY"

easily worked up but cannot recognize their anger

- Allow them to express their anger but try to help them understand the cause of it. This may mean private conversation outside the group
- Identify with any valid point you think they are making and invite the group to respond positively

7 THE "RED HERRING" FISHER

constantly side-tracking discussions so that others forget the point

- Say, "Can we follow that one up later? What about the question we were asking . . .?"
- Face the fact that you're "off the track" and repeat the original question

8 **THE JOKER**
   may be joking to hide embarrassment or to
   relieve some other tension
● Join in the joke but then bring the group
   back to the discussion
● When the humour is misplaced, ignore the
   comment and move the discussion on

9 **THE "DEVIL'S ADVOCATE"**
   consistently presenting opposition even
   when it appears contrived
● They may in fact identify with the view
   being expressed, or they may be doing it on
   behalf of someone else. It is a relatively safe
   way of testing opinion. Try asking if they
   are simply "flying a kite" or whether they
   are genuinely concerned.
● Open up the discussion for the group to
   respond on the subject.

Group work

● Sharing—"Ask people to share a few words which describe
   their week" (page 40)
● **or**—Share practical suggestions as to what being obedient to
   Christ means in daily living (page 40)
● Group Bible study: Luke 5.1-10 (page 40—41).

A continuing strategy

The next step

New Christians need gradually to be incorporated into the local church. So the members of the nurture group need to be given introductions to the wider fellowship. This can happen

● through Sunday worship
● through combined meetings of the nurture groups (see page 11)

There are several options open to those planning the structures that will follow a short nurture group course:

● Pass the new Christians on to some kind of membership class. In different denominations this might mean baptism preparation, confirmation, or membership courses.

● Incorporate the new Christians into your existing system of home groups. Ask yourself whether they are suitable for young Christians to join or whether you need to change them in some way.

● Keep the group together and develop a programme to help members continue to grow in their relationship to God, understanding the Bible, prayer, being committed to one another and the church, and reaching out to those beyond the church with practical caring and the Good News of Jesus.

What kind of groups?

Small groups are just as important in this next stage of growth. In fact, they are important for every stage, because we all need the openness and support that are possible only in a small community of people committed to one another.

The groups to which our new Christians would eventually belong would probably be longer term, continuing groups, and would provide for subsequent stages in Christian growth.

● They are more **Word-centred**—Christ the living Word is worshipped and the written Word, the Bible, which shows us our Lord Jesus Christ, is studied and applied to life.

● Learning how to **pray** and intercessory prayer play a major part in group life.

● The development of **deep relationships** is given special attention. Openness, honesty, sharing, trust, and sensitivity all have an important role in building relationships. Working together on particular acts of service will help keep the group fresh and vital.

- They are basic building blocks for extending Christ's kingdom. Groups should be aiming to grow to the point where they can divide to form two new groups. Where this process repeats itself local churches will, under God, experience new life.

Establishing a continuing programme of evangelism

The new Christians in your nurture group are an important element in the future evangelism of your church. They are likely to have a higher proportion of friends and relatives who are not Christians than the established member, and their fresh experience means that they are powerful and enthusiastic witnesses. They can be shining examples to the rest of the church.

Growing churches are involved in evangelism at a congregational level not as a special "one off" event, but as a way of life. If your church has not thought out its policy in this area, here are some possibilities for you to consider.

1   ARRANGE A COURSE ON PERSONAL WITNESS AND EVANGELISM

Every Christian is called to be a witness and some are gifted as evangelists. Everyone needs help in explaining their faith to others and particular evangelistic gifts need to be identified, developed, and provided with outlets if they are to be exercised properly in the church. *Care to Say Something?* (Scripture Union) or *Tell What God Has Done* (Bible Society) would provide the basis for a course.

2   ENCOURAGE INFORMAL GATHERINGS FOR OUTREACH

Small groups can be used as a first introduction to Christianity. Individuals offer friendship to neighbours and workmates, providing an opportunity for listening, sharing, serving, and discussing issues of common interest. Often they can be just social occasions, with the possibility of spending time in conversation about life and the Christian faith.

3   DEVELOP A SERIES OF EVANGELISTIC HOME MEETINGS

These follow on from the informal gatherings. They are special opportunities to introduce people to Jesus Christ and say something about the Good News.

4   ORGANIZE CONGREGATIONAL EVANGELISTIC EVENTS
This will mean identifying those on the fringe of the church
and developing plans to reach them. Most churches have
- "members" who never attend church worship
- parents of Sunday School children
- husbands of the members of "young wives" groups
- relatives and friends of new Christians

A whole range of events is possible, including
- guest services
- "at homes"
- special programmes planned by the organizations to
  which these people are loosely attached.

Group work
- Group Bible study: Luke 24.36-53 (page 42)
- Discussion: What steps will you take to help the new
  Christians when the nurture group course is completed?

Plenary session
- Share the ideas which came out of your group discussion.
- Discuss any questions or problems people have with plans for
  the nurture groups and deal with any remaining practical
  details.
- Spend some time praying for one another and the work you
  will do.

Living as a Christian

Guidelines for leaders and core members

Nurture course objectives

1   To get to know one another.
2   To ensure that spiritual foundations are properly laid.
3   To encourage Bible reading.
4   To develop the confidence to begin to pray aloud.
5   To enable group members to begin to share their faith.

Beginning

Goals

1   To create a friendly atmosphere in which people feel relaxed and appreciated.

2   To talk about our desire to follow Christ—the shared experience which has brought the group into being.

3   To present what it means to become a Christian, so that everyone has a clear understanding of the step they have taken.

WELCOME

Help everyone feel a sense of warmth and love by being friendly and outgoing. Have the core members briefly introduce their friends to others in the group. Respond thoughtfully and ask questions to show your interest.

Show you are genuinely pleased to have them present. Include latecomers in the group with the minimum of fuss—this could be helped by having spare chairs available.

GETTING ACQUAINTED (30 mins)

(N.B. All activities are suggestions and can be changed to suit the group. You ought to be aiming for the same goals, however.)

Supply paper and pencil for each person. Pair off the group. Try to have a partner yourself if possible and see that married couples or close friends are not put together.

One person seeks to discover as much as possible about the other in 2–3 minutes. Then the process is reversed.

Write out the list below on a piece of paper for each person, or on large paper for all to see. (Other suitable questions can be found in *Creative Ideas for Small Groups*, page 179.)

1   Your name
2   Where you live
3   Some details about your family
4   Your hobbies, interests, sports
5   Where you lived when 10 years old
6   One thing you do well or enjoy doing

PURPOSE

Give a brief explanation of the purpose of the group meeting together.

SHARING (30 mins)

It is helpful for new Christians to talk about their commitment to Christ and clarify what they have done. Allow plenty of time for general sharing. This will play an important role in helping the new Christians build confidence in expressing their faith.

Ask some of the following questions of the whole group and let individuals respond at will. Encourage shy members to share but don't force them. Display an attitude of acceptance to all answers. Avoid lengthy comments by yourself or others.

It is important to encourage a positive atmosphere. Even if new Christians have had poor experiences (*e.g.* of church), do not emphasize them or join in the general criticism. Be positive.

● Can you think of one word to describe how you felt when you decided to follow Christ?
● What had helped you take this step?
● What differences has it made?

TALK (15 mins)

It is essential that everyone understands the steps involved in committing their life to Jesus Christ. It is important that new Christians in your group clearly understand what they have done.

The talk "Beginning as a Christian disciple", on the next pages, will help. Be sure to keep it simple.

PRAYER (5 mins)

The leader makes some suggestions for prayer based on the previous sharing. Try making suggestions singly, allowing time for people to respond in the silence. Don't let the total time run for more than 3 to 5 minutes. The leader closes with a **brief** audible prayer.

REFRESHMENTS

Keep yourself free from preparing refreshments but help distribute them. This will be an important part of the nurture group experience, but do keep it simple so that no one in the group will feel inadequate if their home is used in the future.

Close the "formal" meeting on time; do not let it drag on. Informal conversation can continue afterwards, of course, but everyone must feel free to go when they wish.

NEXT WEEK

1 Encourage new Christians to begin reading Luke's Gospel. As they read, they might like to circle or mark one verse that can be shared with the group next time. Refer especially to the passage for study next week: Luke 23.39-49.

2   Encourage people to feel free to contact the "helper" or nurture group leader if support or help is needed.

3   Specify the day, time, and place of next meeting.

(Did you achieve your goals? If not, what action do you need to take?)

Beginning as a Christian disciple

(For use in session 1)

(This talk takes no longer than 15 minutes if it is carefully prepared and visuals are used. Although overhead projector acetates, prepared in advance, are probably the best way to present the material, plain paper and a felt pen are quite adequate in a small group.)

1   God loves us and made us for a close relationship with himself

● God created us "to be like himself" (Genesis 1.27) which gives us both status and responsibilities in the world God created. One way in which we are "like God" is in having moral and spiritual capacities—we are far more than mere animals.

● God created us capable of knowing him.

● But God didn't create puppets. He made us capable of choosing between good and evil.

This circle could be taken to represent how God made us—his potential for humankind.

2   We have not become what God intended

● The original intimate relationship with God (Genesis 3.8) has been broken right from the beginning of the human race.

● Now we choose naturally not to live God's way. "Everyone has sinned, everyone falls short of the beauty of God's plan" (Romans 3.23, J. B. Phillips).

This warped circle could represent the distortion of God's potential for humankind by the impact of sin from within and from outside. This allows the "world" to "squeeze" us "into its own mould" (Romans 12.2, J. B. Phillips).

3   God did for us through Jesus Christ what we could never do for ourselves

● Because God loves us he made it possible for us to have our close relationship with him restored.

● "Christ is the visible likeness of the invisible God" (Colossians 1.15).

- Through Jesus Christ, God dealt with the problem of sin which prevented us from being "like himself" and spoilt our relationship with him.

"God has shown us how much he loves us—it was while we were still sinners that Christ died for us!" (Romans 5.8).

- When we accept what Christ has done, our relationship with God is restored. From this relationship we now have the power to become what God intended us to be.

"The secret is simply this: Christ **in you**! Yes, Christ **in you** bringing with him the hope of all the glorious things to come" (Colossians 1.27, J. B. Phillips).

4 We need to receive what God offers in Christ

- We must desire to have our broken relationship with God restored, be sorry for our attitude of rebellion and by faith accept Christ and what he has done.

- We often refer to this step as making our "commitment" to Christ. We trust Christ to save us from sin and commit ourselves to his kingly rule over our lives. We are then "born again"—made alive in Christ (John 3.16).

- Christ becomes the focal point around which our life begins to revolve.

Christ, the hidden centre of our lives (Colossians 3.4, J. B. Phillips).

5 Disciples of Christ have a new power within them

- The Holy Spirit of God gives us new spiritual resources which help us to overcome those influences of evil which have spoilt our life.

- The Holy Spirit gives us a new perspective on life and deepens our relationship with God.

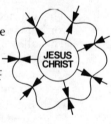

- We don't have to try to make a success of our new Christian life on our own. It is a partnership, with God as the senior partner.

"I have the strength to face all conditions by the power that Christ gives me" (Philippians 4.13).

6   Our relationship with God needs to be maintained

● For any relationship to grow one needs to spend time with the other person. In our relationship with God this is achieved by **prayer, and by knowing and understanding the Bible. It also grows through fellowship**—all that the community of God's people experience and share together in worship, celebration of the sacraments, mission, and service. And we grow by learning to **obey** God—following his leading and intention for each aspect of our life.

Another way of expressing this could be to take the model of a simple wheel. If the hub is Christ and we are the rim, we keep in contact with him through the spokes.

We could also express this by seeing each of the ways we maintain our relationship with God likened to those things which are essential for a new-born baby to grow and mature.

PRAYER

—**Air** (A hymn writer calls prayer "the Christian's vital breath")

BIBLE

—**Food**

FELLOWSHIP

—**A Family** where care, support, sharing, and love are experienced

OBEDIENCE

—**Exercise** to help us develop and keep fit and healthy

Being sure

Goals

1   To share **positive** experiences of life in general.
2   To share how God's promises are being fulfilled in our lives.
3   To appreciate how Jesus cares for each one of us, guiding and protecting us in daily living.

GETTING TO KNOW EACH OTHER (15 mins)

Display the following uncompleted sentences for all to see. Give each person a minute or two to think of responses. Then, taking one question at a time, go round the group and let each person give responses.

●   One of the nicest things that has ever happened to me is . . .
●   A part of creation which inspires me is . . .
●   The person who has helped me most in my life is . . .

Check how the group members are feeling about sharing something of themselves. Conclude by making a brief observation about how they have shared important feelings about themselves, and yet have not been threatened.

This is part of the positive experience of a Christian group.

SING OR LISTEN (5 mins)

Hymns/songs if appropriate, **or** a suitable track or two from a Christian record.

OPTION A (20 mins)

Encourage each person to share one verse from their daily reading of Luke's Gospel that is particularly meaningful to them. Accept each person's comment and encourage them in their discovery.
Try hard not to preach a sermon to them!

OPTION B (20 mins)

We want Christians to learn to trust God and what he says to us through the Bible.

Talk for a few minutes about what God has promised for our lives with him. You can use some of the promises in Luke's Gospel (1.54; 4.16-21 and 7.21-23; 11.9-13; 23.42-43; 24.45-49) or from elsewhere in the Bible (*e.g.* John 3.16; 14.15-17; 1 John 1.9).

Optional questions:

●   In what experiences or circumstances of life have you been most aware of your need for God's help?

- What changes have begun to take place which show that God is at work in your life?

GROUP BIBLE STUDY (45 mins)
Luke 23.39-49

Give a **brief** introduction explaining that reading whole incidents and sections of Scripture, not just isolated verses, is an important stimulus to growth. Point out that in different ways people we read about in the Bible were sure about God.

Give people time to write answers to the following questions. Then let different group members give answers to each question. Don't discuss them until each person has shared on each question. Be encouraging to each person as they contribute.

1 What did the army officer think about Jesus? How could he have been so sure?

2 In verse 46 what word best describes Jesus' attitude to his Father?

   Doubting   Bitter
   Confident   Resigned

   If you were going through a difficult time how might Jesus' example help you?

3 What did Jesus promise the dying thief in verse 43? How would you have felt if you had been the thief?

4 Jesus accepted, loved, and forgave a man who was condemned as a criminal. What does that say to you about his attitude towards you?

   After members have given the answers to these questions, ask:

- Which particular answer is most challenging at this time and which is most encouraging?

PRAYER (3 mins)
Each prays silently for the people sitting on either side, recalling the things which they found challenging and encouraging.

NEXT WEEK
Encourage members to continue reading Luke's Gospel and to come next week prepared to share a significant verse.
Especially note Luke 8.4-15 for next week's session.

(Remember to follow up those who didn't attend or who need help. Did you achieve your goals? If not, what action do you need to take?)

3 Growing

Goals

1   To be open with each other about the need for personal help and growth.

2   To give examples of how our thinking has developed and our faith has been stretched, and how we have been led to a greater trust in the Lord Jesus.

GETTING TO KNOW EACH OTHER (15 mins)

1   Form pairs, each with someone not known very well, and have each person take 2 minutes to tell their partner four things about themselves from these areas: likes and dislikes, strengths and weaknesses, fears and joys, successes and failures.

2   In the group, have each person introduce their partner by saying, "One thing I have discovered about . . . is . . ."

OPTION A (20 mins)

Encourage each person to share one verse that is particularly meaningful from their daily readings in Luke's Gospel.

Optional questions:

● What has God been showing you from his Word in the last few days?

● What has God been doing in your life?

OPTION B (20 mins)

Spend a few minutes talking about personal prayer and Bible reading.

Suggested activities or questions:

● What problems have you had in reading the Bible? List them on one side of a chart.

● How may these be overcome?
Discuss and write possible solutions/suggestions next to each problem.

● What time do you feel would suit you best to pray and read the Bible?

PRAYER (15 mins)

Encourage members to list one or two things they could pray about under each of the following headings:

| praise | thanks | family |
| confession | others | yourself |

Use these ideas to form single-word or one sentence prayers for a time of prayer.

Invite members to pray aloud. Emphasize that, though this may be new to them, there is no reason to be embarrassed. It will be a new experience for other members of the group too. And God is more interested in us than in special words.

GROUP BIBLE STUDY (40 mins)

Luke 8.4-15

Ask someone to read the passage (it's better if they can be prepared beforehand—suddenly being asked can be threatening, especially to those who don't read too well).

Then ask members to look into the passage and jot down answers to these questions.

1   Verse 12: once we have heard the truth about Jesus what might make us forget it? How could we guard against that?

2   Verse 13: we all feel tempted at some point to go back on our commitment or to wonder whether anything has really happened. Have members of the group already faced this? How can we help one another keep our faith and joy alive?

3   Verse 14: list what the thorns might be in your life.

4   Verse 15: what must we do if we are to grow properly?

5   What changes will you want to make in your life as a result of today's reading?

NEXT WEEK

1   Encourage members to continue reading Luke's Gospel and to come prepared to share a significant verse.

2   Ask them to read Luke 5.1-10 in preparation for the next Bible study.

3   Ask for two volunteers from the new Christians to read Luke 5.1-10 in next week's meeting. Each will read from a different translation. Encourage them to practise it beforehand.

(Does someone need to be followed up after the meeting? Did you achieve your goals? If not, what action do you need to take?)

4 Being obedient

Goals

1   To emphasize the need to live a life of continuing obedience to Christ.

2   To share specific examples of what obedience has meant to us in our daily lives.

3   To learn from Christ's example that obedience entails humble service towards each other and to all in need.

SHARING (10 mins)

- Ask people to share a few words which describe their week.
- Ask them to share a helpful verse from their reading of Luke's Gospel.

SING OR READ (5 mins)

Hymns or songs, if appropriate, or read a psalm of praise, *e.g.* Psalms 145–150 (from a modern translation).
In either case, have group members underline phrases that enlighten or inspire them.

PRAYER

Members read these phrases as their prayer.

OPTION A (20 mins)

Share verses from Bible readings that are particularly meaningful and helpful. Encourage members to explain how God has spoken to them about some area of their life.

OPTION B

Spend a few minutes talking about what it means to obey Christ in our daily lives. You could use John 14.15-17 again (see Option B in Session 2), emphasizing the obedience that accompanies the promise, or John 13.34-35 and Luke 6.46-49.

Ask members for practical suggestions on what being obedient to Christ means in daily living (leave time for this).

GROUP BIBLE STUDY (45 mins)

Luke 5.1-10

This study will help the new Christian grapple with one specific and demanding area of obedience.

The persons selected last week read the Scripture passage from the two different translations. Allow a period for silent reflection after each reading.

Ask members to complete the following statements individually in silence and then share responses with the group, one section at a time.

1   If I had been Peter my reaction to the large, unexpected catch
would have been one of amazement, excitement, unworthiness,
irritation, confusion or . . .

2   I think Jesus did this to
    a) help Peter become a great leader
    b) help him trust God more
    c) make him feel unworthy
    d) help him obey Jesus even when he didn't understand
    e) show him that being obedient brings rewards
    f) . . . .

3   Catching men involves
    a) telling them about Jesus
    b) showing love and concern for them
    c) helping to meet any needs they have
    d) encouraging them to become members of the church
    e) . . . .

4   Think of one person you would like to bring to Jesus. What
practical steps might you take?

5   What are some of the things obedience will involve in the
situations group members face this week? List some on paper.

REFLECTION AND PRAYER (10 mins)

Following the above discussion, ask members to make some
resolution concerning the way in which they will obey Christ during
the following week. This should be written on a piece of paper and
kept by each member.

Indicate that time will be allowed next week for any to share how
they have put this into practice during the week.

A time of silent prayer could follow, with the leader closing with a
brief prayer.

NEXT WEEK

1   If group members are still reading Luke's Gospel encourage
them to continue reading, and come prepared to share a
significant and helpful verse.

2   By this week, some may have finished reading Luke's Gospel.
Now is a good time to introduce them to a systematic Bible
reading programme. Have copies of programmes available (see
page 46).

3   Ask members to read Luke 24.36-53 in preparation for next
week's study.

(Does someone need to be followed up? Did you achieve your
goals? If not, what action do you need to take?)

5 Being established

Goals

1   To teach practical skills in understanding and applying a Bible passage.

2   To encourage new Christians to share their new-found faith with their family and friends.

3   To pray for individuals and situations with which we are concerned.

SHARING (20 mins)

● Anyone may share how they put into practice what they learnt last week, or a helpful verse from Luke's Gospel.

● In what ways have members known God's strength as they have tried to obey him during the week?

GROUP BIBLE STUDY (45 mins)

Luke 24.36-53

The passage may be read aloud either by the leader, using expression, or by the group as a whole so that they are all involved.

Individual study of the passage follows for 10 minutes, each person using the three symbols pictured below. Explain the symbols before the study and make sure everyone has a copy of the symbols and their explanation. Each person is to mark the margin of their Gospel or Bible with the appropriate symbol—in pencil if preferred.

 This part throws new light on a subject or shows me something I have not realized before.

This challenges me in some way or pricks my conscience.

? I do not understand this word, phrase, or verse, or I do not agree with it.

The members come together to share their marking of symbols, one at a time. Have them share their reasons for marking verses or phrases.

Go through the study yourself and be prepared to share your reactions first, if necessary. Prepare the passage beforehand by studying it in some depth.

Write a summary of your corporate findings on paper at the end.

SING (5 mins)

Hymns or songs related to the Bible study, or other favourites.

OPTION A (30 mins)

Talk about sharing our faith with our families and friends.

- Are there any particular persons with whom you would like to share your experience of Christ?
- What are the problems you face in sharing Christ with these people?
- How can some of these problems be overcome?

OPTION B (30 mins)

Share how individual Bible reading and prayer is going, and any other aspects of life as a Christian the group members may wish to raise.

Encourage all to participate (without pressure). Try to have the group supply answers and help each other rather than do it all yourself.

PRAYER (10 mins)

Chain prayer—each briefly prays for the person on their left, bearing in mind particular needs which may have arisen during the Bible study or sharing. If a person prefers to pray silently they say "Amen" audibly at the end so the next person knows when to pray.

NEXT WEEK

1   Encourage Bible reading and prayer.
2   Refer members to Luke 12.4-12 which is the passage for Bible study in the next session.

(Does anyone need to be followed up? Did you achieve your goals? If not, what action do you need to take?)

6 Continuing

Goals

1   To alert new Christians to the fact that the Christian life will sometimes be "tough going".

2   To clarify the role of the Holy Spirit in the believer's life.

3   To decide what further steps should be taken now that the nurture course has been completed.

SHARING (10 mins)

Use one of the following statements and ask members to complete it.

- The thing I have enjoyed most about our meetings is . . .
- The area in my life where I am most aware of growth is . . .

PRAYER (5 mins)

Worship, adoration, praise, and thanksgiving related to the sharing time or assisted by a hymn, song, or record.

GROUP BIBLE STUDY (40 mins)

Luke 12.4-12

1   What does this passage warn Christians to expect as they live in obedience to Christ?

2   In what ways do we experience this today? Give some specific examples.

3   What comfort does Jesus offer to his followers in these situations?

4   How does this help us in relation to the examples given in question 2?

Be prepared to give further clarification of the role of the Holy Spirit in the believer's life, particularly as explained by Jesus in this passage. This may be most appropriately done in relation to question 3.

WHERE DO I GO FROM HERE? (15 mins)

- Individual reflection—what specific action can I take to enable me to continue to grow as a Christian?
- Sharing of plans in groups of two or three to help each other see what these plans might involve—both the problems and the benefits.
- Brief time of prayer in these groups to ask for God's help.

WHERE DO WE GO FROM HERE?

- Encourage people to express their ideas about meeting in a group in the future.

- Brainstorm any ideas—when, where, how long meetings should last, what sort of group, and what to do in the group.
- Explore the options. Remember to keep in mind other church programmes and plans.
- Write up on paper a clear plan of what is going to happen from now on.

(Did you achieve your goals? If not, what action do you need to take?)

Read through Luke in thirty days

Day

Resources

Christian belief

John Balchin	*What Christians Believe* (Lion)
Richard Bewes and Robert Hicks	*The Pocket Handbook of Christian Truth* (Creative Publishing)
Andrew Knowles	*Finding Faith* (Lion)
John Stott	*Basic Christianity* (IVP)

Christian living

Michael Green	*New Life, New Lifestyle* (Hodder)
Andrew Knowles	*Real-Life Christianity* (Lion)
David Watson	*Live a New Life* (IVP)
John White	*The Fight* (IVP)
Derek Williams	*The Pocket Handbook of Christian Living* (Creative Publishing)
David Winwood	*I Want to Begin a Christian Life* (MAYC)

Biographies are also good books to lend to new Christians.

Bible reading

Some of the organizations that publish different types of Bible-reading materials for individuals:

Bible Reading Fellowship
Bible Society
Crusade for World Revival
International Bible Reading Association
Inter-Varsity Press
Salvation Army
Scripture Union

Group Bible study

Some of the organizations that publish group Bible study materials:

Bible Reading Fellowship
Bible Society
Campus Crusade for Christ
Celebration Services
Church Pastoral Aid Society
Navigators
Scripture Union
SEAN (Study by Extension for All Nations)

Groups

Eddie Gibbs	*Grow Through Groups* (Grove Books)
Jean Grigor	*Grow to Love* (St Andrew's Press)
Jean Grigor	*A Tool For Christians* (Social Responsibility Committee of the Church of Scotland)

Roberta Hestenes	*Using the Bible in Groups* (Bible Society)
John Mallison	*Building Small Groups* (SU)
John Mallison	*Creative Ideas for Small Groups* (SU)
Ron Trudinger	*Cells For Life* (Olive Tree Publications)
Albert J. Wollen	*God at Work in Small Groups* (SU)

Evangelism

Paul Little	*How To Give Away Your Faith* (IVP)
Rebecca Manley Pippert	*Out of the Saltshaker* (IVP)
Roy Pointer	*Tell What God Has Done* (Bible Society)
Gavin Reid	*Good News To Share* (Falcon)
Michael Wooderson	*Good News Down The Street* (Grove Books)
	Care To Say Something? (SU/Mission England)

You should be able to get the books you need in your local Christian bookshop or, in case of difficulty, direct from the publishers.